the World's Best Funny Rhymes

BY JOSEPH ROSENBLOOM
ILLUSTRATIONS BY JOYCE BEHR

 Sterling Publishing Co., Inc. New York

Library of Congress Cataloging-in-Publication Data

Rosenbloom, Joseph.
   [Silly verse (and even worse)]
   The world's best funny rhymes / by Joseph Rosenbloom ;
illustrations by Joyce Behr.
     p.   cm.
   Originally published under title: Silly verse (and even worse).
   Includes index.
   Summary: Contains more than 200 short, humorous poems from
anonymous sources.
   ISBN 0-8069-6968-7
   1. Children's poetry.   2. Children's poetry, American.
3. Humorous poetry.   4. Humorous poetry, American.   [1. Humorous
poetry.   2. American poetry—Collections.   3. Poetry—Collections.]
   I. Behr, Joyce, ill.   II. Title.
PN6109.R67   1989
808.81'7—dc19   88-13937
                                           CIP
                                           AC

Published in 1988 by Sterling Publishing Co., Inc.
Two Park Avenue, New York, N.Y. 10016.
Originally published by Sterling Publishing Co., Inc.
under the title "Silly Verse (and Even Worse)"
copyright © 1979 by Joseph Rosenbloom
Distributed in Canada by Oak Tree Press Ltd.
% Canadian Manda Group, P.O. Box 920, Station U
Toronto, Ontario, Canada M8Z 5P9
Distributed in Great Britain and Europe by Cassell PLC
Artillery House, Artillery Row, London SW1P 1RT, England
Distributed in Australia by Capricorn Ltd.
P.O. Box 665, Lane Cove, NSW 2066
Manufactured in the United States of America
All rights reserved

To Julie Backerman
with love

Books by Joseph Rosenbloom

Biggest Riddle Book in the World
Daffy Definitions
Doctor Knock-Knock's Official Knock-Knock
  Dictionary
Funniest Dinosaur Book Ever!
Funniest Joke Book Ever!
Funniest Knock-Knock Book Ever!
Funniest Riddle Book Ever!
Funny Insults & Snappy Put-Downs
Gigantic Joke Book
Giggles, Gags & Groaners
Knock-Knock! Who's There?
Looniest Limerick Book in the World
Mad Scientist
Monster Madness
Nutty Knock Knocks!
Official Wild West Joke Book
Perfect Put-Downs & Instant Insults
Ridiculous Nicholas Haunted House Riddles
Ridiculous Nicholas Pet Riddles
Ridiculous Nicholas Riddle Book
696 Silly School Jokes & Riddles
Spooky Riddles & Jokes
Wacky Insults and Terrible Jokes
World's Best Sports Riddles & Jokes
Zaniest Riddle Book in the World

Contents

Contents

1 Glub, Glub, Glub

Connie, Connie

Connie, Connie in the tub,
She forgot to use the plug.
Oh, my heavens! Oh, my soul!
There goes Connie down the hole!
    Glub, glub, glub . . .

Every Time I Take a Bath

Giving me a washing machine
Was very nice of you,
But every time I take a bath
It beats me black and blue.

Phoebe (rhymes with Beebee)

A certain young chap named Bill Beebee
Was in love with a lady named Phoebe.
    "But," said he, "I must see
    What the license fee be
Before Phoebe be Phoebe B. Beebee."

To the Household's Disgust

There was an old lady in Rye
Who was baked by mistake in a pie.
    To the household's disgust,
    She emerged through the crust
And exclaimed, with a yawn,
    "Where am I?"

Going Tomorrow

A traveller once to his sorrow
Requested a ticket to Morrow.
    Said the agent, "It's plain
    That there isn't a train
To Morrow today, but tomorrow!"

A Young Lady Named Hannah

There was a young lady named Hannah
Who slipped on a peel of banana.
    She wanted to swear,
    But her mother was there,
So she whistled "The Star-Spangled
    Banner."

A gentleman passing (named Keller)
Picked up her brown gloves and umbrella.
    "Did you fall, ma'am?" he cried.
    "Do you think," she replied,
"I lay down for the fun of it, fella?"

A Fly and a Flea in a Flue

A fly and a flea in a flue
Were imprisoned, so what could they do?
    Said the fly, "Let us flee!"
    "Let us fly!" said the flea,
And they flew through a flaw in the flue.

A Young Lady of Lynn

There was a young lady of Lynn
Who was so excessively thin
    That when she essayed
    To drink lemonade
She slipped through the straw and fell in.

A Young Man Called O'Toole

There was a young man called O'Toole,
Who thought he was handsome and cool.
    He grew a long beard
    And then, as I feared,
Tripped on it and fell in the pool.

They'll Send You to Jail

A maiden caught stealing a dahlia,
Said, "Oh, you shan't tell on me,
    shahlia?"
    But the florist was hot.
    He said, "Like it or not,
They'll send you to jail, you bad gahlia."

A Phantom Named Pete

There once was a phantom named Pete,
Who never would play, drink or eat.
    He said, "I don't care
    For a Coke or eclair.
Can't you see that I'm dead on my feet?"

Shot or Not?

Ned Nott was shot
   and Sam Shott was not.
So it is better to be Shott
   than Nott.

Some say Nott
   was not shot,
But Shott says
   he shot Nott.

Either the shot Shott shot at Nott
   was not shot
   or
Nott was shot.

If the shot Shott shot shot Nott,
   Nott was shot.
But if the shot Shott shot shot Shott,
   then Shott was shot,
   not Nott.

However,
   the shot Shott shot shot not Shott—
but Nott.

Ezra Shank

He rocked the boat,
Did Ezra Shank.
These bubbles mark
            o
            o
            o
            o
            o
Where Ezra Sank.

As for the Bucket

There was an old man of Nantucket,
Who kept all his cash in a bucket.
    But his daughter, named Nan,
    Ran away with a man,
And as for the bucket—Nantucket.

He followed the pair to Pawtucket,
The man and the girl with the bucket,
    And he said to the man,
    "You're welcome to Nan,"
But as for the bucket—Pawtucket.

The pair tracked Paw back to Manhasset,
Where he still had the cash as an asset.
    And Nan and the man
    Stole the money and ran,
And as for the bucket—Manhasset.

2 Open Other End

Those Nasty Words

I wrestle with cardboard,
I struggle with foil.
I pluck at tiny tabs until
My blood begins to boil.
And when I'm all for giving up
On this I can depend—
I see those nasty, spiteful words:
"Open Other End."

My Teacher Loves Me

My teacher loves me, thinks I'm dear.
She's kept me for the fourth straight year.

Clean Sweaters

Nothing attracts
Mustard from wieners
As quickly as sweaters
Just back from the cleaners.

The Thing That Couldn't Be Done

Somebody said that it couldn't be done—
    But he, with a smile, replied
That he'd never say it couldn't be done
    Anyway, not till he'd tried.
So he buckled right in, and he led with his
    chin;
    By golly, he went right to it!
He tackled The Thing That Couldn't Be
    Done!
    And he couldn't do it.

An Old Man from Peru

There was an old man from Peru
Who dreamt he was eating his shoe.
    He awoke in the night
    In a terrible fright,
And found it was perfectly true.

Beg Your Pardon

Some rabbits came over from Arden
And gobbled up most of my garden.
   They feasted for hours
   On stalks and on flowers
And never once said, "Beg your pardon."

The Loan

I think that I shall never see
The dollar that I loaned to thee;
A dollar that I could have spent
On many forms of merriment—
The one I loaned to you so gladly—
The same one that I need so badly—
For whose return I had great hope,
Just like an optimistic dope.
For dollars loaned to folks like thee
Are not returned to fools like me.

So I'm Told

I shot a sneeze into the air.
It fell to earth, I know not where.
But some time later, so I'm told,
Twenty others caught my cold.

P.S.

I shot an arrow into the air.
It fell to earth I know not where.
P.S. I lose a lot of arrows that way.

Dusted and Busted

A maid with a duster
Made a furious bluster,
Dusting a bust in the hall.
When the bust it was dusted,
The bust it was busted.
The bust it was dust, and that's all.

The Joke

The joke you just told isn't funny one bit.
It's pointless and dull, wholly lacking in
    wit.
It's so old and stale, it's beginning to
    smell!
Besides, it's the one I was going to tell.

Hard Hard Hard

It's hard to lose a friend
When your heart is full of hope;
But it's worse to lose a towel
When your eyes are full of soap.

An Apple a Day

There once was a fellow named Roderick
    Gray,
Who ate apples all night
    and ate apples all day.
    He is now in a hospital,
    That's what they say,
And a doctor a day keeps the apple away.

Shy

There was a young girl of Shanghai
Who was so incredibly shy,
    She almost turned blue
    When she said, "How'd you do,"
And blushed when she whispered,
    "Good-bye."

The Wondrous Deep

Behold the wondrous mighty deep
Where crabs and lobsters learn to creep,
And little fishes learn to swim,
And scuba divers tumble in.

No Horse Could Be Found

A major, with wonderful force,
Called out in Hyde Park for a horse.
    All the flowers looked round,
    But no horse could be found,
So he just rhododendron, of course.

3 I Thought I Heard a Chicken Sneeze

He Sneezed So Hard

Out in the garden, pickin' peas,
I thought I heard a chicken sneeze.
He sneezed so hard with whoopin' cough,
He sneezed his head and tail right off.

I Saw a Man

Yesterday upon the stair
I saw a man who wasn't there.
He wasn't there again today.
I really wish he'd go away!

Marguerite

A centipede named Marguerite
Bought shoes for each one of her feet.
"For," she said, "I might chance
To go to a dance,
And I must have my outfit complete."

A Young Lady from Woosester

There was a young lady from Woosester
Who ussessed to crow like a roosester.
    She ussessed to climb
    Seven trees as a time—
But her sisister ussessed to boosester.

The 2:02 (The Two-Two)

There was a young lady named Sue,
Who wanted to catch the 2:02.
    Said the trainman, "Don't hurry
    Or flurry or worry;
It's a minute or two to 2:02."

Miss Dowd

A mouse in her room woke Miss Dowd.
She was frightened and screamed very
    loud.
    Then a happy thought hit her:
    To scare off the critter,
She sat up in bed and meowed.

Crows and Roosters

I sometimes think I'd rather crow
And be a rooster than to roost
And be a crow.
But I dunno.

A rooster he can roost also,
Which doesn't seem fair when crows can't
    crow
Which may help some.
Still I dunno.

Crows should be glad of one thing, though:
Nobody thinks of eating crow,
While roosters are quite good enough
For anyone, unless they're tough.

There are lots of tough old roosters,
    though,
And anyway, a crow can't crow,
So maybe roosters have more to show.
It looks that way.
But I dunno.

A Fine Tale

I had a little chicken,
    The smartest ever seen.
She washed up the dishes
    And kept the house clean.
She went to the mill
    To fetch me some flour,
And always got home
    In less than an hour.
She baked my bread,
    She changed my crib,
And never mentioned
    Chicken lib.

Mary's Parrot

Mary had a parrot.
She killed it in a rage.
For every time her boyfriend came,
The darn thing told her age.

A Wise Old Owl

A wise old owl sat on an oak.
The more he saw, the less he spoke.
The less he spoke, the more he heard—
Why can't we be like that old bird?

Wouldn't Lay an Egg

Had a little chicky,
It wouldn't lay an egg.
Poured hot water
Up and down its leg.
Little chicky cried,
Little chicky begged,
Little chicky laid
A hard-boiled egg.

My Poem

That poem is a splendid thing;
I love to hear you quote it.
I love the thought; I like the swing.
I like it all. (I wrote it!)

My Nose

It doesn't breathe; it doesn't smell;
It doesn't feel so very well.
I am disgusted with my nose.
The only thing it does is blows.

The Poets Sing

The poets sing
Concerning spring
And say the bird
Is on the wing.

Upon my word,
That is absurd,
Because the wing
Is on the bird.

4 Bad Habits

How Passionate!

I know a girl named Passion.
I asked her for a date.
I took her out to dinner
And gosh! How Passionate!

Never Again

Here I sit in the moonlight,
Abandoned by women and men,
Muttering over and over,
"I'll never eat onions again."

An Old Man of Calcutta

There was an old man of Calcutta,
Who spoke with a terrible stutter.
    At breakfast he said,
    "Give me b-b-b-bread,
And b-b-b-b-b-b-butter."

A Girl We Know

A girl we know, Rosie De Fleet,
Is so very unusually neat,
    She washes all day
    To keep microbes away
And wears rubber gloves just to eat.

A Fat Lady from Skye
(rhymes with *pie*)

There was a fat lady from Skye
Who was sure she was going to die,
    But for fear that once dead
    She would not be well-fed,
She gulped down a pig, a cow, a sheep,
    twelve buns, a seven-layer cake, four
    cups of coffee and a green apple pie.

**Odd Fellow of Tyre
(rhymes with *fire*)**

There was an odd fellow of Tyre,
Who constantly sat on the fire.
    When asked, "Are you hot?"
    He said, "Certainly not,
I'm James Winterbottom, Esquire."

Somewhat Alike

The gum-chewing student,
The cud-chewing cow,
Are somewhat alike,
Yet different somehow.
Just what is the difference—
I think I know now—
It's the thoughtful look
On the face of the cow.

'Twas the Night Before . . .

The stockings were hung
By the chimney with care.
I had worn them for weeks
And they needed the air.

I've Done It All My Life

I eat my peas with honey;
I've done it all my life.
It may seem kind of funny,
But it keeps them on my knife.

You Lazy Sinner

Get up, get up, you lazy head,
    Get up, you lazy sinner.
We need those sheets for tablecloths,
    It's nearly time for dinner.

Owen More

Did you ever hear
    This tale before
About that chap
    Named Owen More?

Well, Owen More,
    He went away
Owen More
    Than he could pay.

He just came back
    From some far shore.
I hear he still is
    Owen More.

Pamela Penn

A girl name of Pamela Penn
Just loved to get married to men,
    Not once, but again
    And again and again,
And again and again and again.

A Young Girl from Asturias
(rhymes with *furious*)

There was a young girl from Asturias,
Whose temper was frantic and furious.
    She used to throw eggs
    At her grandmother's legs—
A habit unpleasant but curious.

She's Now Gone to Rest

There was an old girl of Genoa
    (Jen-OH-ah),
I blush when I think what Iowa
    (Eye-OH-ah).
      She's gone now to rest—
      I guess that's for the best,
Or else I would borrow Samoa.

You Never Can Tell

There was a young maid who said, "Why
Can't I look in my ear with my eye?
      If I put my mind to it,
      I'm sure I can do it!
You never can tell till you try."

5 Be Kind to the Moose

The Moose

Be kind to the moose.
He may be of use,
For hanging your hat
Or something like that . . .

Don't Worry

Don't worry if your grades are low
And your rewards are few.
Remember that the mighty oak
Was once a nut like you.

The Wizard of Oz

The fabulous Wizard of Oz
Retired from business becoz
    What with up-to-date science
    To most of his clients
He wasn't the wiz that he woz.

A Sleeper

A sleeper from the Amazon
Put nighties of his grandma's on.
    The reason? That
    He was too fat
To get his own pajamazon.

A Young Man of Aberdeen

A young man of fair Aberdeen
Once grew so remarkably lean,
    So flat and compressed,
    That his back touched his chest,
And sideways he couldn't be seen.

A Young Lady Named Rose

There was a young lady named Rose,
Who had a huge wart on her nose.
    When she had it removed,
    Her appearance improved,
But her glasses slipped down to her toes.

Wright Wrote

A right-handed fellow named Wright
In writing "write" always wrote "rite"
    Where he meant to write right.
    If he'd written "write" right,
Wright would not have wrought rot writing
    "rite."

I'm Thor!

The thunder god went for a ride
Upon his favorite filly.
    "I'm Thor," he cried,
    And the horse replied,
"You forgot your thaddle, thilly."

Down the Street

Down the street his funeral goes
As sobs and wails diminish.
He died from drinking straight shellac,
But he had a lovely finish.

Which Way Did She Go?

An elephant living in Kent
Had a nose that was terribly bent.
   She followed her nose
   One day, I suppose,
And no one knows which way she went.

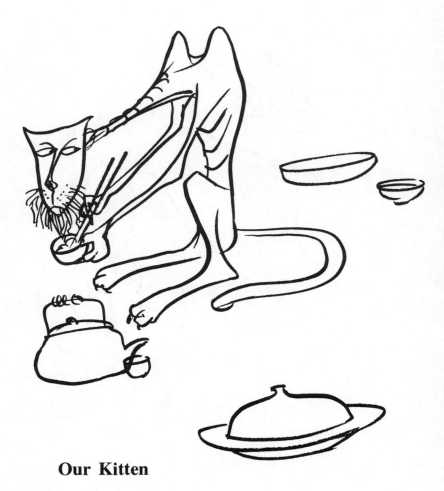

Our Kitten

Our kitten, the one we call Louie,
Will never eat liver so chewy,
    Nor the milk, nor the fish
    That we put in his dish.
He only will dine on chop suey.

I Love to Do My Homework

I love to do my homework,
It makes me feel so good.
I love to do exactly
As my teacher says I should.

I love to do my homework,
I never miss a day.
I even love the men in white
Who are taking me away.

The Shy Shrimps' Song

Should a shad, shelling shrimps for a
        shark,
Cease to shuck the shamed shrimps, who
        remark,
        "Serve us not without dressing!
        'Tis really distressing!"
Or should he just shuck the shrimps in the
        dark?

Common Scents

The porcupine may have his quills,
    The elephant his trunk;
But when it comes to common scents,
    My money's on the skunk.

The Cheerful Bear

A cheerful old bear at the zoo
Could always find something to do.
    When it bored him, you know,
    To walk to and fro,
He reversed it and walked fro and to.

A Hunter Named Shepherd

They tell of a hunter named Shepherd
Who was eaten for lunch by a leopard.
    Said the leopard, "Egad,
    You'd be tastier, lad,
If you had been salted and peppered."

That's Okay

Early to bed,
Early to rise,
That's okay
For other guys.

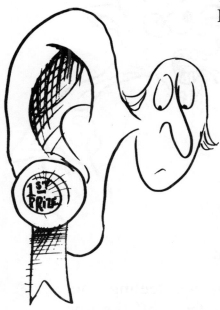

A Young Man of Devizes
(rhymes with *sizes*)

There was a young man of Devizes,
Whose ears were of different sizes.
    One was so small
    It was no use at all,
But the other was huge and won prizes.

Old Hogan's Goat

Old Hogan's goat was feeling fine,
Ate six red shirts from off the line.
Old Hogan grabbed him by the back
And tied him to the railroad track.

Now as the train came into sight,
That goat grew pale and green with fright.
He heaved a sigh as if in pain,
Coughed up those shirts and flagged the
    train.

The Headlight

The lightning bug is bright,
But it hasn't any mind.
It blunders on through life
With a headlight on behind.

Song: "My Bonnie"

My Bonnie looked into the gas tank,
But nothing she could see;
She lighted a match to assist her—
Oh, bring back my Bonnie to me!

An Old Sweetheart

I offered him a sausage
But the dog said, "I decline,
For in that little sausage
Is an old sweetheart of mine!"

A Dog Is Loved

A dog is loved
    By old and young.
He wags his tail
    And not his tongue.

Fuzzy Wuzzy

Fuzzy Wuzzy wuz a bear.
Fuzzy Wuzzy had no hair.
Fuzzy Wuzzy wuzn't fuzzy,
—Wuz he?

Jokes

I'm fairly gracious to the bore
    Who tells me jokes I've heard before.
But he will find me glum and grim
    Who tells me jokes I've told to him.

6 You're Sitting on My Head

You're Sitting on My Head

I was sitting on a tombstone,
When a ghost came by and said,
"I'm sorry to disturb you,
But you're sitting on my head."

Last Night

The Eskimo sleeps on his white bearskin,
And sleeps rather well, I'm told.
Last night I slept in my little bearskin,
And caught a terrible cold.

City Rhymes

Said little Johnnie to the Owl,
    "I've heard you're wondrous wise,
And so I'd like to question you;
    Now, please don't tell me lies.

"The first thing that I'd have you tell,
    My empty mind to fill,
Could it have been some rotten beef
    That made Chicago, Ill.?

"I've heard it said, yet do not know—
    In fact, it may be bosh—
Tell me, is it lots of dirt
    That makes Seattle, Wash.?

"This is a time of rising debts,
    As you must surely know.
This secret please impart to me:
    How much does Cleveland, O.?

"Of history you've learned so much,
    Much more than many men.
So tell me in a whisper, please,
    When was Miss Nashville, Tenn.?

"Some voices are so strong and full,
    And some so still and small,
I've often wondered, sir,
    How loud could Denver, Col.?"

The Owl scratched his feathered head.
    "I'm sorry, little man.
Ask someone else. I cannot tell.
    Perhaps Topeka, Kan."

The Eeriest Fight

A skeleton from far Khartoum
Invited a ghost to his room.
   They spent the whole night
   In the eeriest fight
As to who should be frightened of whom.

A Young Man of Fort Worth

There was a young man of Fort Worth,
Who was born on the day of his birth.
    He was married, some say,
    On his wife's wedding day,
And he died when he quitted the earth.

The 4:04 (The Four-Four)

"There's a train at 4:04," said Miss Jenny.
"Four tickets I'll take; have you any?"
    Said the man at the door,
    "Not four for 4:04,
For four for 4:04 is too many."

Friendly and Waggy

There was a small maiden named Maggie,
Whose dog was enormous and shaggy.
    The front end of him
    Looked vicious and grim,
But the tail end was friendly and waggy.

The Tin Whistle

I bought a tin whistle,
But it wooden whistle.
I bought a steel whistle,
But it steel wouldn't whistle.
So I bought a tin whistle,
And now I tin whistle.

The Pun

"A pun is the lowest form of wit."
It does not tax your brain a bit.
You merely take a word that's plain
And pick out one that sounds the same.

Perhaps some letter may be changed,
Or others slightly disarranged;
This gives the meaning some new twist,
Which may delight the humorist.

Here's a sample which may show
The way a good pun ought to go:
"It isn't the cough that carries you off,
It's the coffin they carry you off in."

Three Fellows from Gary

There once were three fellows from Gary
Named Larry and Harry and Barry.
 Now Harry was bare
 As an egg or a pear,
But Larry and Barry were hairy.

Who Was It?

Someone started the whole day wrong,
Someone robbed the day of its song,
    Was it you? (Too true.)
Someone started the day a-right,
Someone made it happy and bright,
    Do you know about it? (I doubt it.)

Maggie Rose

You'd do the same
    As Maggie Rose.
You'd be no different,
    I suppose.
For when she sat
    Upon a tack,
Maggie Rose.

7 Humpy and Grumpy

Tomorrow's Test

Now I lay me down to rest,
I pray I pass tomorrow's test.
If I should die before I wake,
That's one less test I'll have to take.

What's Swat

Nothing makes one hotter
Than wielding a fly-swatter.
But, alas, it's all we've got
To teach those silly flies what's swat.

The Camel

If you—all your life—had been humpy
And swayed over sand, lank and lumpy,
  You'd probably be
  Exactly like me—
Though perhaps you'd be even more
  grumpy.

Don't Shout!

I raised such a hullaballoo
When I found a big mouse in my stew;
    Said the waiter, "Don't shout
    And wave it about
Or the rest will be wanting one, too!"

The New Gnu

There was a sightseer named Sue,
Who saw a strange beast at the zoo.
    When she asked, "Is it old?"
    She was smilingly told,
"It's not an old beast, but a gnu."

The Short Harp Player

There once was a very fat carp
Who wanted to play on a harp.
    But to his chagrin
    So short was his fin
He couldn't reach up to C sharp.

What Some People Do

Jibber, jabber, gabble, babble,
Cackle, clack and prate,
Twiddle, twaddle, mutter, stutter,
Utter, splutter, blate . . .

Chatter, patter, tattle, prattle,
Chew the rag and crack,
Spiel and spout and spit it out,
Tell the world and quack . . .

Sniffle, snuffle, drawl and bawl,
Snicker, snort and snap,
Bark and buzz and yap and yelp,
Chin and chirp and chat . . .

Shout and shoot and gargle, gasp,
Gab and gag and groan,
Hem and haw and work the jaw,
Grumble, mumble, moan . . .

Beef and bellyache and bat,
Say a mouthful, squawk,
That is what some people do
When they merely talk.

No-Pocket Complaint

I wish I were a kangaroo,
Despite its funny stances.
I'd have a place to put my junk
When I go out to dances.

A Cat in Despondency

A cat in despondency sighed
And resolved to commit suicide.
    She passed under the wheels
    Of eight automobiles,
And under the ninth one she died.

The Weigher

The man stood on the weighing machine
In the light of lingering day.
A counterfeit coin he dropped in,
And silently stole a weigh.

Pop Bottles

Pop bottles pop-bottles in pop shops.
The pop-bottles Pop bottles poor Pop
    drops.
When Pop drops pop-bottles, pop-bottles
    plop.
When pop-bottles topple, Pop mops slop.

The Finished Speaker

I love a finished speaker,
I really, really do.
I don't mean one who's polished,
I do mean one who's through.

Anna Elise

Anna Elise, she jumped with surprise.
The surprise was so quick, it played her a
  trick.
The trick was so rare, she jumped on a
  chair.
The chair was so frail, she jumped into a
  pail.
The pail was so wet, she jumped into a net.
The net was so small, she jumped on a
  ball.
The ball was so round, she jumped on the
  ground,
And ever since then, she's been turning
  around.

A Farmer from Stratton

A nearsighted farmer from Stratton
Would sit all through church
    with his hat on.
  "If I wake up," he said,
  "With my hat on my head,
I'll know that it hasn't been sat on."

The Zombie's Tears

A zombie who thought he was dying
Just couldn't seem to stop crying,
    Until his friend said,
    "You're already quite dead."
Then the zombie's tears began drying.

First Kiss

I remember—I remember well—
The first girl that I kissed.
She closed her eyes, I closed mine,
And then—worst luck—we missed!

Two Dead Men

One fine day in the middle of the night,
Two dead men got up to fight.
Back to back they faced each other,
Drew their swords and shot each other.
A frozen donkey, passing by,
Kicked a blind man in the eye,
Knocked him through a nine-inch wall
Into a ditch and drowned them all.

8 Modern Nursery Rhymes

Humpty Dumpty

Humpty Dumpty sat on a wall,
Humpty Dumpty had a great fall.
All the king's horses and all the king's men
Had scrambled eggs for breakfast again.

Jack Be Nimble

Jack be nimble, Jack be quick.
Jack, stand still; you're making me sick!

Mary Had a Little Lamb

Mary had a little lamb,
'Twas awful dumb, it's true.
It followed her in a traffic jam,
And now it's mutton stew.

Mary had a little lamb
As dirty as a hog.
They asked her how it got that way.
She answered simply, "Smog."

Mary had a little lamb,
Her father shot it dead.
Now Mary takes her lamb to school
Between two hunks of bread.

More About Mary

Mary had a little lamb,
And tied him to a heater.
And every time he turned around,
He burned his little seater.

Mary had a little lamb,
She set it on the shelf;
And every time it wagged its tail,
It spanked its little self.

The Animals

Mary had a little lamb;
Freddie had a pup;
Ronnie had a crocodile.
It ate the others up.

Little Bo-Peep

Little Bo-Peep has lost her sheep
And looks for them sedately.
I hope that she will find them soon;
We've had no lamb chops lately.

Jack and Jill

Jack and Jill went up the hill
To fetch a pail of water.
Jack fell down and broke his crown
So he couldn't play king anymore.

Little Jack Horner

Little Jack Horner
Sat in a corner,
Watching the girls go by.
Along came a beauty
And he said, "Hi, cutie!"
And that's how he got a black eye.

Fleas

Some folks say that fleas are black,
But I know that's not so,
'Cause Mary had a little lamb
With fleas as white as snow.

Old Mother Hubbard

Old Mother Hubbard went to the
    cupboard,
To get her dog a banana.
When she got there, the cupboard was
    bare,
So the poor dog had to eat sponge cake.

Little Miss Muffet

Little Miss Muffet sat on a tuffet,
Eating her curds and whey.
Along came a spider who sat down beside
    her
And said, "Whatcha got in the bowl,
    sweetheart?"

Little Miss Muffet sat on a tuffet,
Eating her curds and whey.
Along came a spider who sat down beside
    her
And said, "Is this seat taken?"

Hickory, Dickory, Dock

Hickory, dickory, dock,
The mice ran up the clock,
The clock struck one;
The others escaped with minor injuries.

Still More About Mary

Mary had a little lamb,
    A lobster and some prunes,
A glass of milk, a piece of pie,
    And then some macaroons.

It made the busy waiters grin
    To see her order so,
And when they carried Mary out,
    Her face was white as snow.

9 Don't Spit on the Floor

When I Die

When I die, bury me deep,
Bury my history book at my feet.
Tell the teacher I've gone to rest,
And won't be back for the history test.

Message for Doctors

A doctor fell into a well
And broke his collarbone.
A doctor should attend the sick
And leave the well alone.

Gallons of Ink

There's a clever old miser who tries
Every method to e-con-o-mize.
    He says, with a wink,
    "I save gallons of ink
By simply not dotting the I's."

The Umbrella

There was a young lady of Spain,
Who couldn't go out in the rain,
    'Cause she'd lent her umbrella
    To Queen Isabella
Who never returned it again.

A Cannibal of Penzance
(rhymes with *aunts*)

A cannibal bold of Penzance
Ate an uncle and two of his aunts,
    A cow and her calf,
    An ox and a half—
And now he can't button his pants.

A Young Lady of Crete
(rhymes with *neat*)

There was a young lady of Crete
Who was so exceedingly neat,
    When she got out of bed,
    She stood on her head
To make sure of not soiling her feet.

I Flunked, Too

Roses are red,
Violets are blue.
I copied your paper,
And I flunked, too.

It Cooled Her Off

She wore her stockings inside out
    All through the summer heat.
She said it cooled her off to turn
    The hose upon her feet.

Don't Spit on the Floor

There was a young fellow of Wheeling,
Endowed with such delicate feeling,
    When he read on the door,
    "Don't spit on the floor,"
He jumped up and spat on the ceiling.

Spot

I had a pup, his name was Spot.
And when we cooked, he licked the pot.
And when we ate, he never forgot
To lick the dishes. Thanks a lot!

One Fine October Morning

One fine October morning
    In September, last July,
The moon lay thick upon the ground,
    The snow shone in the sky.
The flowers were singing gaily,
    And the birds were in full bloom.
I went down to the cellar
    To sweep the upstairs room.

It's Laughable

It always makes me laugh,
It's so wonderful a treat,
To see an athlete run a mile
And only move two feet.

Accident-prone

Joe, Joe, stubbed his toe
On the way to Mexico.
In Brazil he hurt his back,
Sliding on the railroad track.
When he got home he broke a bone,
Talking on the telephone.

Song: "Home on the Range"

"Oh, give me a home,
Where the buffalo roam,
And the cowboys work till they drop.
Where the cows all relax
And lie flat on their backs,
And this brings the cream to the top."

10 Done to Death by a Banana

In Memory of Anna

Here lies the body of Anna,
Done to death by a banana.
It wasn't the fruit that laid her low,
But the skin of the thing that made her go.

Toot! Toot!

A peanut sat on the railroad track;
Its heart was all aflutter.
Along then came the 8:15—
Toot! Toot! Peanut butter.

A Lady from Guam

There once was a lady from Guam
Who said, "Now the ocean's so calm
    I will swim, for a lark."
    She encountered a shark.
Let us now sing the 90th psalm.

Apple Cider

There was a young lady who tried
A diet of apples, and died.
    The unfortunate miss
    Really perished of this:
Too much cider inside her inside.

A Young Man Named Paul

There once was a young man named Paul
Who went to a fancy dress ball.
    He thought he would risk it
    And go as a biscuit,
But a dog ate him up in the hall.

Nice Little Cat

There was a young man from the city,
Who met what he thought was a kitty.
    He gave it a pat,
      And said, "Nice little cat!"
And they buried his clothes out of pity.

If You Should Meet a Crocodile

If you should meet a crocodile
    Don't take a stick and poke him
Ignore the welcome in his smile,
    Be careful not to stroke him.
For as he sleeps upon the Nile,
    He gets thinner and thinner.
So when you meet a crocodile
    He's ready for his dinner.

When He Awoke

There was a young person named Ned
Who dined before going to bed
    On lobster and ham
    And salad and jam,
And when he awoke he was dead.

As Was His Desire

There was a young fellow named Greer
Who hadn't an atom of fear.
    He touched a live wire,
    As was his desire,
(Most any old line will do here.)

She Ended Like This

Suzanna, a sweet little miss,
Believed roller skating was bliss.
    But she knew not her fate,
    For a wheel off her skate
Flew off and she ended like this!

Our Old Friend

We had an old friend name of Skinner
Who said, "How I wish I were thinner!"
    He lived for three weeks
    On a grape and two leeks.
We think of him Sundays at dinner.

One Summer at Tea

There was a young parson named Perkins,
Exceedingly fond of small gherkins.
    One summer at tea
    He ate forty-three,
Which pickled his internal workin's.

Spring and Fall

There was a young fellow named Hall,
Who fell in the spring in the fall.
    'Twould have been a sad thing
    If he died in the spring,
But he didn't—he died in the fall.

Ruth and Johnnie

Ruth and Johnnie
    Side by side,
Went out for an
    Auto ride.
They hit a bump,
    Ruth hit a tree,
And John kept going
    Ruthlessly.

Short Story

Little Willie;
Pair of skates;
Hole in the ice;
Golden Gates.

11 I Don't Care!

My Head Fell Off

As I was going out one day,
My head fell off and rolled away.
But when I saw that it was gone,
I picked it up and put it on.

And when I got into the street,
A fellow cried, "Look at your feet!"
I looked at them and sadly said,
"I've left them both asleep in bed."

I Don't Care

Teddy on the railroad,
Picking up stones.
Along came an engine,
And broke Teddy's bones.
"Oh," said Teddy,
"That's no fair."
"Oh," said the engineer,
"I don't care."

You Told Me Once

Do you love me,
Or do you not?
You told me once,
But I forgot.

No Lock or Key

The elephant carries a big trunk;
He never packs it with clothes.
It has no lock and it has no key,
But he takes it wherever he goes.

Wonderful Bird

A wonderful bird is the sea gull,
It can fly quite as high as an eagle.
    It will sit on the sand,
    And sometimes will stand,
But you can't tell a he from a she gull.

A Window Cry

Oh, I've paddled on the ocean,
I've tramped upon the plain.
But I never saw a window cry
Because it had a pane.

Go, My Son

"Go, my son, and shut the shutter."
This I heard a mother utter.
"Shutter's shut," her son did mutter.
"I can't shut 'er any shutter."

Noah's Ark

When Noah sailed the waters blue,
He had his troubles, same as you.
For forty days he drove his ark
Before he found a place to park.

Three Young Rats

Three young rats with black felt hats,
Three young ducks with baseball bats,
Three young dogs with cowboy boots,
Three young cats in warm-up suits,
Went out to walk with two young pigs
In satin vests and fluffy wigs;
But suddenly it chanced to rain
And so they all went home again.

There Was a Cat

Long ago there was a cat,
Who swallowed a ball of yarn;
And when the cat had kittens,
They all had sweaters on.

Fate's Peculiar Ways

I often stop and wonder
At Fate's peculiar ways:
So many of our famous men
Were born on holidays.

Deafer with Zephyr

A farmer once called his cow "Zephyr."
She seemed such a breezy young hephyr.
   When the farmer drew near,
   She kicked off his ear,
And now the old farmer's much dephyr.

One of Those Days . . .

Did you ever go fishing on a bright sunny
day—
Sit on a fence and have the fence give
way?
Slide off the fence and rip your pants—
And see the little fishes do a
hootchy-kootchy dance?

No Tail At All

The squirrel has a bushy tail;
The possum's tail is bare;
The rabbit has no tail at all,
Just a little bunch of hair.

All the Little Sausages

One day a boy went walking.
He walked into a store.
He bought a pound of sausage,
And laid it on the floor.

The boy began to whistle.
He whistled up a tune,
And all the little sausages
Went dancing round the room.

As I Looked Out

As I looked out on Saturday last,
A fat little pig went hurrying past.
Over his shoulders he wore a shawl,
Although it didn't seem cold at all.
I waved to him, but he didn't see,
For he never so much as looked at me.

Once again, when the moon was high,
I saw that pig come hurrying by.
Back he came at a terrible pace.
The moonlight shone on his little pink face,
And he smiled with a smile that was quite
content.
But I never knew where that little pig
went.

Bug in a Jug

Curious fly,
Vinegar jug,
Slippery edge,
Pickled bug.

The Very Last Word

Here
again is
one of those
triangles. The
idea is not particu-
larly new, but yet it
is amazing how, despite its
staleness and lack of humor, most
everyone will read this all the way down
to the very last letter in the very last word.

12 Why Doesn't It Rain on You?

Song: "Good Morning to You"

Good morning to you,
Good morning to you.
You look very drowsy,
In fact, you look lousy.
Is that any way
To start out the day?

I Love You So Well

I love you, I love you,
I love you so well,
If I had a peanut,
I'd give you the shell.

I Love You

I love you, I love you,
I love you, I do.
But don't get excited,
I love monkeys, too.

True Love

I love you, I love you,
Be my valentine.
And give me your bubble gum—
You're sitting on mine.

Drip Drip Drip

Every time it rains,
I think of you:
    Drip . . . drip . . . drip . . .

To Scare Away the Mice

I wish I had your picture,
It would be very nice.
I'd hang it in the attic
To scare away the mice.

You and I

Here's to you: so good you are.
Here's to me: so bad I am.
But as good as you are
    And as bad as I am—
I'm as good as you are—
    As bad as I am!

Why Doesn't It Rain On You?

The rain makes everything beautiful,
It makes the flowers blue.
If the rain makes everything beautiful,
Why doesn't it rain on you?

The Little Doughnut

Your father is a baker;
Your mother cuts the bread;
And you're the little doughnut
With a hole right through your head.

I Wish I Were a Dozen Eggs

I wish I were a dozen eggs
    Sitting in a tree;
And when you passed along below
    I'd splatter you with me.

I Wish I Were a Grapefruit

I wish I were a grapefruit,
And here's the reason why:
When you came to eat me,
I'd squirt you in the eye!

Roses Are Red

Roses are red,
Violets are blue.
Umbrellas get lost,
Why don't you?

Moldy Cheese

Go on to college, gather your knowledge,
Study and worry and stew.
If they make penicillin from moldy cheese,
They can make something good
    out of you.

13 Ouch!

Ough!

While a baker was kneading his dough,
A muffin fell right on his tough.
He suddenly howled, "Ough!"
Because it hurt him sough.

If I Get Fresh

I love me so; I think I'm grand.
I go to the movies and hold my hand.
I put my arm around my waist.
If I get fresh, I slap my face.

A Cowboy Called Slouch

So tall was a cowboy called Slouch,
He was taller than most—in a crouch!
    When a horse stomped his toe,
    The pain had so far to go,
It took him three days to say "Ouch!"

A Young Lady of Leeds

There was a young lady of Leeds,
Who swallowed six packets of seeds.
    In a month, silly lass,
    She was covered with grass,
And she couldn't sit down for the weeds.

Betty at the Party

"When I was at the party,"
    Said Betty, aged just four,
"A little girl fell off her chair
    Right down upon the floor.
And all the other little girls
    Began to laugh, but me—
I didn't laugh a single bit,"
    Said Betty seriously.

"Why not?" her mother asked her,
    Full of delight to find
That Betty—bless her little heart!—
    Had been so sweet and kind.
"Why didn't you laugh, my darling?
    Or don't you like to tell?"
"I didn't laugh," said Betty,
    "'Cause I'm the one who fell."

I'll Be Darned!

Said the toe to the sock,
    "Let me through, let me through!"
Said the sock to the toe,
    "I'll be darned if I do."

Mislaid False Teeth

There once was an old man named Keith,
Who mislaid his pair of false teeth,
    Laid them down on a chair,
    Forgot they were there,
Sat down and was bitten beneath.

She Cut Off His Head

There was an old lady of Wooster
Who was often disturbed by a rooster.
    She cut off his head
    To make sure he was dead,
And now he can't crow like he use-ter.

He's Got Fleas

I've got a dog as thin as a rail,
He's got fleas all over his tail.
Every time his tail goes flop,
The fleas on the bottom
All hop to the top.

What Santa Needs

When in frosty midnight,
He cruises through the air,
What Santa needs for Christmas
Is fur-lined underwear.

But when sliding down the chimney
Toward the fire that we tend
Asbestos pants for Santa
Would be better in the end.

The Slippery Slide

Down the slippery slide they slid,
    Sitting slightly sideways,
Slipping swiftly, see them skid
    On holidays and Fridays.

As Red as a Rose

There once was a fellow named Moses
Who went out to pick some red roses.
He slipped on his toes and fell on his nose,
And red as a rose now his nose is.

I Lay Me Down

Now I lay me down to sleep,
A bag of candy at my feet.
If I should die before I wake,
You'll know I died of stomach ache.

Little Jerry

For asking lots of questions
Little Jerry has a flair.
His weary parents say he is
Their little question heir.

The Tail

I had a little pig,
I fed him in a trough.
He got so fat
His tail dropped off.

So I got me a hammer
And I got me a nail,
And I made my little pig
A brand new tail.

If I Were an Apple

If I were an apple
    And grew on a tree,
I'd ripen and fall
    On a good kid like me.

I wouldn't stay high,
    Giving nobody joy.
I'd drop to the ground
    And say, "Eat me, my boy!"

Lullaby

Rock-a-bye, baby,
In the treetop.
Don't you fall out—
It's a very big drop.

That Good-For-Nothing Donkey

My mother bought a donkey—
She thought it was a cow.
She sent me out to milk it,
But I didn't know how.
The night was dark and cloudy.
Alas, I couldn't see,
And that good-for-nothing donkey
Took a big bite out of me.

The Water Basin

There was a king and he had three
    daughters
And they all lived in a basin of water.
    The basin is bended,
    My story is ended.
If the basin had been stronger,
My story would've been longer.

14 It's a Dark, Dark World

Raising Frogs

Raising frogs for profit
Is a very sorry joke.
How can you make money
When so many of them croak?

History Is Dead

History's a dreadful subject,
Dead as it can be.
Once it killed the Romans
And now it's killing me.

Never Say Die!

There was an old man named McGuire,
Who stumbled and fell in the mire.
    Said a man passing by,
     "Cheer up; never say die!"
"But I have to," he cried, "I'm a dyer!"

Trying to Get to Harvard

Two little boys late one night
Tried to get to Harvard on the end of a
    kite.
The kite string broke
And down they fell.
Instead of going to Harvard,
They went to _____.

Now don't get excited,
And don't get pale.
Instead of going to Harvard,
They went to Yale.

A Little Green Vampire

A little green vampire
In his little green way
Some little green apples
Devoured one day.
And the little green grass
Now tenderly waves
O'er the little green vampire's
Green little grave.

If a Skunk Went to College

Roses are red,
Violets are blue,
If a skunk went to college
He'd go to P.U.

Oh, Nuts!

Starlight, star bright,
First star I see tonight,
I wish I may, I wish I might—
Oh, nuts, it's just a satellite . . .

Starlight, star bright,
First star I see tonight,
I'd like to fly, I'd like to go—
Oh nuts, it's just a UFO . . .

The Weather

Whether the weather be fine
    Or whether the weather be not,
Whether the weather be cold
    Or whether the weather be hot,
We'll weather the weather,
    Whatever the weather,
Whether we like it or not.

It's a Dark, Dark World

In the dark, dark world,
    there's a dark, dark country.
In the dark, dark country,
    there's a dark, dark forest.
In the dark, dark forest,
    there's a dark, dark house.
In the dark, dark house,
    there's a man trying to find a fuse.

Mr. Inside and Mr. Outside

Mr. Inside went over to see Mr. Outside.
Mr. Inside stood outside and called to
  Mr. Outside inside.
Mr. Outside answered Mr. Inside from
  inside
And told Mr. Inside to come inside.
Mr. Inside said, "No," for Mr. Outside
  to come outside.

Mr. Outside and Mr. Inside argued from
  inside and outside
About going outside or coming inside.

Finally, Mr. Inside coaxed Mr. Outside
  to come outside
Instead of Mr. Outside having Mr. Inside
  come inside.
Then both Mr. Outside and Mr. Inside
Went to the riverside and committed
  suicide.

You Can't Trap Mother Nature

If you build a better mousetrap
And put it in your house,
Before long, Mother Nature's
Going to build a better mouse.

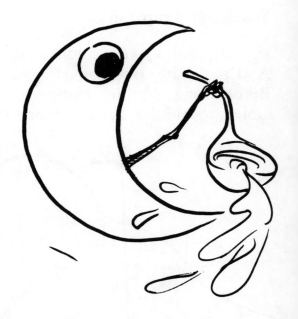

The Man in the Moon

The Man in the Moon, as he sails the sky,
    Is a very remarkable skipper,
But he made a mistake when he tried to
    take
    A swallow or two from the Dipper.
He dipped into the Milky Way,
    And slowly and carefully filled it.
The Big Bear growled and the Little Bear
    howled
And scared him so much that he spilled it.

I'm Glad

I'm glad the sky is painted blue
And the earth is painted green.
You'd never know it, though,
With all the smog that's in between.

Have You Ever Seen?

Have you ever seen a sheet on a river bed?
Or a single hair from a hammer's head?
Has the foot of a mountain any toes?
And is there a pair of garden hose?

Does the needle ever wink its eye?
Why doesn't the wing of building fly?
Can you tickle the ribs of a parasol?
Or open the trunk of a tree at all?

Are the teeth of a rake ever going to bite?
Have the hands of a clock any left or right?
Can the garden plot be deep and dark?
And what is the sound of the birch's bark?

He Spoke the Truth

"Your teeth are like the stars," he said,
And pressed her hand so white.
He spoke the truth, for like the stars,
Her teeth came out at night.

Who Knows?

Who knows when the sky may fall,
And with a calm grin squash us all!
We ought to think of our poor souls,
And not wear underwear with holes.